C000016593

SEAFOOD

RECIPE

COOKBOOK

+50 Fresh & Delicious Recipes to Maintain a Healthy Weight

Ally Rogers

All rights reserved.

Disclaimer

The information contained i is meant to serve as a comprehensive collection of strategies that the author of this eBook has done research about. Summaries, strategies, tips and tricks are only recommendation by the author, and reading this eBook will not guarantee that one's results will exactly mirror the author's results. The author of the eBook has made all reasonable effort to provide current and accurate information for the readers of the eBook. The author and it's associates will not be held liable for any unintentional error or omissions that may be found. The material in the eBook may include information by third parties. Third party materials comprise of opinions expressed by their owners. As such, the author of the eBook does not assume responsibility or liability for any third party material or opinions. Whether because of the progression of the internet, or the unforeseen changes in company policy and editorial submission guidelines, what is stated as fact at the time of this writing may become outdated or inapplicable later.

The eBook is copyright © 2021 with all rights reserved. It is illegal to redistribute, copy, or create derivative work from this eBook whole or in part. No parts of this report may be reproduced or retransmitted in any reproduced or retransmitted in any forms whatsoever without the writing expressed and signed permission from the author.

INTRODUCTION

There are few things in life that taste as delish and divine on your tongue as a freshly cooked or an expertly prepared lobster, shrimp dish or plate of tuna. If you've never known the taste of crab or seafood that melts in your mouth, head out now and grab yourself a bite.

As a big plus, eating seafood can help prevent heart attacks and strokes, can lower blood pressure and may even help ward off depression. Regular fish consumption reduces the risk of heart attack by as much as 40 percent. Seafood's magic ingredient: omega-3 fatty acids. Fatty fish, like salmon (fresh and canned), tuna (fresh and canned), herring, trout, mackerel and sardines, are loaded with these beneficial fats. Just be careful with cooking; pan-frying and deep-frying at high temperatures can destroy omega-3 fats.

There are so many tasty ways to incorporate seafood into your meal prep. It's a healthy and delicious way to eat lean, filling protein, and a backbone of the Mediterranean diet. We are thrilled to bring you a collection of the best of the best fish and seafood recipes!

The recipes below include salmon, shrimp, scallops, octopus and Haddock. Each recipe is healthy, relatively easy to make, and full of incredible flavor. In fact, there are so many favorites here that we couldn't narrow it down. There's a little something for everyone, from shrimp fried rice to pesto salmon to perfectly seared scallops.

SHRIMP

Spicy grilled shrimp

Serves 6

Ingredients

- 1/3 cup olive oil
- 1/4 cup sesame oil
- 1/4 cup fresh parsley-chopped
- 3 Tablespoons Spicy Chipotle BBQ Sauce
- 1 Tablespoon minced garlic
- 1 Tablespoon Asian Chile Sauce
- 1 teaspoon salt
- 1 teaspoon black pepper
- 3 Tablespoons lemon juice
- 2 lbs. large shrimp, peeled and de-veined
- 12 wooden skewers, soaked in water
- Rubbing

Cooking Directions

Whisk together the olive oil, sesame oil, parsley, Spicy Chipotle BBQ Sauce, minced garlic, Chile sauce, salt, pepper, and lemon juice in a mixing bowl. Set aside about 1/3 of this marinade to use while grilling.

Place the shrimp in a large, re-sealable plastic bag. Pour in the remaining marinade and seal the bag.

Refrigerate for 2 hours. Preheat The Good-One®
Grill for high heat. Thread shrimp onto skewers,
piercing once near the tail and once near the head.
Discard marinade.

Lightly oil grill grate. Cook shrimp for 2 minutes
per side until opaque, basting frequently with
reserved marinade

Grilled herbed shrimp

Serves 4

Ingredients

- 2 lbs peeled & deveined jumbo shrimp $\frac{3}{4}$ cup olive oil
- 2 tablespoons freshly squeezed lemon juice 2 cups chopped fresh basil
- 2 garlic cloves, crushed
- 1 tablespoon chopped parsley 1 teaspoon salt
- $\frac{1}{2}$ teaspoon oregano
- $\frac{1}{2}$ teaspoons freshly ground black pepper

Cooking Directions

1. Lay shrimp in a single layer in a shallow glass or ceramic dish.
2. In a food processor, blend the olive oil with the lemon juice.
3. Cover and refrigerate for 2 hours. Stir the shrimp 4 to 5 times during marinating.
4. Prepare the grill.
5. Lightly oil the grilling rack.
6. Lay the shrimp on the oiled rack (can skewer if desired) over the hot coals and grill for 3

to 5 minutes on each side until slightly charred and cooked through. Do not over-cook.

7. Serve immediately.

Shrimp en brochette

Serves 4 (appetizer portions)

These are great appetizers to serve before any meal. You can also substitute bay scallops. You might want to double the recipe because they are so good!

Ingredients

- $\frac{1}{2}$ tablespoon hot sauce
- 1 tablespoon Dijon-style mustard 3 tablespoons beer
- $\frac{1}{2}$ pound large shrimp, peeled and deveined 3 slices bacon, cut lengthwise into 12 strips 2 tablespoons light brown sugar

Cooking Directions

Combine the hot sauce, mustard and beer in mixing bowl.

Add the shrimp and toss to coat evenly. Refrigerate for at lest 2 hours. Drain and reserve the marinade. Wrap each shrimp with a strip of bacon.

Thread 3 shrimp onto 4 double skewers. Put the brochettes in a shallow bowl and pour in the reserved marinade. Sprinkle the shrimp with the sugar. Refrigerate for at least 1 hour.

Prepare Good-One Grill. Place the brochettes on the grill, pour the marinade over them, and close the lid. Cook for 4 minutes, then turn them over, close the lid and cook for 4 minutes.

Serve immediately

Shrimp packets

- 4 lbs Large Shrimp
- 1 Cup Butter or Margarine
- 1 Large Clove Garlic, Minced
- 1/2 tsp black pepper
- 1 tsp salt
- 1 cup parsley, minced

Peel and clean shrimp

Cream butter; add remaining ingredients to the butter and mix well. Cut 6 (9-inch) strips of heavy duty aluminum foil. Then cut each strip in half. Divide shrimp equally on each piece of foil. Top each with 1/12th of the butter mixture, bring foil up around shrimp; twist tightly to seal. Place shrimp packets on embers. Cook 5 minutes.

Makes 12 packets

Basil shrimp

- 2 1/2 tablespoons olive oil
- 1/4 cup butter, melted
- 1/2 lemons, juiced
- tablespoons coarse grained prepared mustard
- ounces minced fresh basil

- cloves garlic, minced
- salt to taste
- 1 pinch white pepper
- 3 pounds fresh shrimp, peeled and deveined

In a shallow, non-porous dish or bowl, mix together olive oil and melted butter. Then stir in lemon juice, mustard, basil and garlic, and season with salt and white pepper. Add shrimp, and toss to coat. Cover, and place in refrigerator or cooler for 1 hour. Preheat grill to high heat. Remove shrimp from marinade, and thread on skewers. Lightly oil grate, and arrange skewers on grill. Cook for 4 minutes, turning once, until done.

Grilled bacon-wrapped shrimp

- 1 lb. large shrimp
- bacon slices, cut in 1/2
- pepper jack cheese

Wash, shell, and devein shrimp. Slit the back of each shrimp. Place a small slice of cheese in the slit and wrap with a piece of bacon. Use a toothpick to hold together. Cook on the grill until bacon is slightly crisp. This is delicious and easy!

Grilled shrimp

- 1 pound medium sized shrimp
- 3-4 tablespoons olive oil
- 2 tablespoons "Old Bay Seasoning"

Peel and devein shrimp, leaving on the tails. Place all ingredients in a zip lock bag and shake well. This can marinade 5 minutes or several hours. Place shrimp on a "grill pan" (with holes so that the shrimp do not fall in between grates on the grill) and grill medium high for several minutes. Very spicy

Serves 2

Alabama Shrimp Bake

- 1 cup butter or margarine, melted
- 3/4 cup lemon juice
- 3/4 cup Worcestershire sauce
- 1 tablespoon salt
- 1 tablespoon coarsely ground pepper
- 1 teaspoon dried rosemary
- 1/8 teaspoon ground red pepper
- 1 tablespoon hot sauce
- 3 garlic cloves, minced
- 2 1/2 pounds unpeeled large or jumbo shrimp
- 2 lemons, thinly sliced
- 1 medium onion, thinly sliced
- Fresh rosemary sprigs

Combine first 9 ingredients in a small bowl; set aside.

Rinse shrimp with cold water; drain well. Layer shrimp, lemon slices, and onion slices in an ungreased 13 x 9 x 2-inch baking dish. Pour butter mixture over shrimp. Bake uncovered, at 400 degrees F for 20 to 25 minutes or until shrimp turn pink, basting occasionally with pan juices. Garnish with fresh rosemary sprigs.

Serves 6.

Almost Shrimp Paesano

- Shrimp
- 1 egg
- 1 cup milk
- Salt and pepper to taste
- 1 pound extra-large shrimp, peeled and deveined, tails left on
- 1/2 cup all-purpose flour
- Vegetable oil

In a shallow bowl, combine eggs, milk, salt and pepper. Dip shrimp in mixture, then dip in flour lightly.

Heat oil in a sauté pan until hot, and then add shrimp 4 to 6 at a time, making sure shrimp have plenty of room to cook. (It's important that shrimp are not near each other or touch.) Brown them on one side, then turn and brown them on the other. Cook until done, or put on a baking sheet in a preheated 350 degrees F oven to finish cooking. Meanwhile, prepare sauce.

Sauce

- 1 1/2 cups (3 sticks) cold butter, cut into 1-inch pieces
- Juice of 1 medium lemon
- 1 clove garlic, minced
- 2 tablespoons minced fresh parsley

In a heavy saucepan, combine butter, lemon juice and garlic. Put over medium-low heat and whisk mixture constantly until the butter is just melted and thickened. Stir in parsley, then remove from heat.

Pool sauce on plate, then top with cooked shrimp

Serves 3 to 4

Bean & Shrimp Risotto

- 1 ½ cups onion, chopped
- 1 lb. peeled, deveined shrimp
- 4 cloves garlic, minced
- 1 cup snap peas
- 1 TBS olive oil
- 1 can kidney beans or ½ cups cooked
- 3 to 4oz. mushrooms, sliced
- dry-package kidney beans, rinsed,
- 1 ½ cups Arborio rice, drained
- 3 cans fat-free reduced-sodium chicken broth
- 1 medium tomato, chopped
- cup Parmesan or Asiago cheese
- salt & pepper to taste

Sauté' onion, garlic, & mushrooms in oil in large saucepan until tender, 5 to 8 Minutes.

Stir in rice and cook 2 to 3 Minutes.

Heat broth to boiling in medium saucepan; reduce heat to low. Add 1 cup broth to rice and cook, stirring constantly, until broth is absorbed, 1 to 2

Minutes. Slowly add 2 cups broth and simmer, stirring, until broth is absorbed.

Add shrimp, snap peas and remaining broth to saucepan. Cook, stirring frequently, until rice is just tender and liquid is absorbed, 5 to 10 Minutes. Add beans and tomatoes; cook 2 to 3 Minutes longer. Stir in cheese; season to taste with salt & pepper.

Beer-Broiled Shrimp

- 3/4 cup Beer
- 3 tablespoons vegetable oil
- 2 tablespoons snipped parsley
- 4 teaspoons Worcestershire sauce
- 1 clove garlic, minced
- 1/2 teaspoon salt
- 1/8 teaspoon pepper
- 2 pounds large shrimp, unshelled

Combine Coors®, oil, parsley, Worcestershire sauce, garlic, salt and pepper. Add shrimp; stir. Cover; let stand at room temperature for 1 hour.

Drain, reserving marinade. Place shrimp on well-greased broiler rack; broil 4 to 5 inches from heat for 4 minutes. Turn; brush with marinade. Broil 2 to 4 minutes more or until bright pink.

Makes 6 servings

Boiled Gulf Shrimp

- 1 gallon water
- 1 (3 ounce) box Zatarain's crab boil

- 2 lemons, sliced
- 6peppercorns
- 2bay leaves
- 5pounds raw shrimp in the shell

Bring to boil the water seasoned with crab boil, lemons, peppercorns and bay leaves. Drop in shrimp. When water returns to a boil, cook jumbo or large shrimp for 12 to 13 minutes and medium shrimp for 7 to 8 minutes. Remove from heat and add 1 quart ice water. Let sit for 10 minutes. Drain.

Serve Rémoulade Sauce as a dip.

Rémoulade Sauce

- 1/2 tablespoon Creole mustard or more
- 2 tablespoons grated onion
- 1 pint mayonnaise
- 1/4 cup horseradish or more
- 1/2 cup chopped chives
- 1/4 teaspoon salt
- 1 tablespoon lemon juice
- 1/4 teaspoon pepper

Mix all ingredients. Serve over cold boiled shrimp for a shrimp rémoulade main course or use as a dip for boiled shrimp. Sauce is best after 24 hours.

Makes 2 1/4 cups sauce.

California Scampi

- 1 pound butter, clarified
- 1 tablespoon minced garlic
- 1 teaspoon salt
- 1 teaspoon pepper
- 1 1/2 pounds large shrimp, shelled and de-veined

Heat 3 tablespoons of the clarified butter in a large skillet. Add garlic and sauté. Add salt and pepper and the shrimp, which can be butterflied, if desired. Sauté until shrimp change color and are tender. Add remaining butter and heat through. Place shrimp on plates and spoon hot butter over.

Makes 4 to 6 servings

Champagne Shrimp And Pasta

- 8 ounces angel hair pasta
- 1 tablespoon extra-virgin olive oil
- 1 cup sliced fresh mushrooms
- 1 pound medium shrimp, peeled and deveined
- 1-1/2 cups champagne
- 1/4 teaspoon salt
- 2 tablespoons minced shallots
- 2 plum tomatoes, diced
- 1 cup heavy cream
- salt and pepper to taste
- 3 tablespoons chopped fresh parsley
- freshly grated Parmesan cheese

Bring a large pot of lightly salted water to a boil. Cook pasta in boiling water for 6 to 8 minutes or until al dente; drain. Meanwhile, heat oil over medium-high heat in a large frying pan. Cook and stir mushrooms in oil until tender. Remove mushrooms from pan, and set aside.

Combine shrimp, champagne, and salt in the frying pan, and cook over high heat. When liquid just begins to boil, remove shrimp from pan. Add shallots and tomatoes to champagne; boil until liquid is reduced to 1/2 cup, about 8 minutes. Stir in 3/4 cup cream; boil until slightly thick, about 1 to 2 minutes. Add shrimp and mushrooms to sauce, and heat through. Adjust seasonings to taste. Toss hot, cooked pasta with remaining 1/4 cup cream and parsley. To serve, spoon shrimp with sauce over pasta, and top with Parmesan cheese.

Coconut Shrimp with Jalapeño Jelly

- 3 cups shredded coconut
- 12 (16–20 or 26–30) shrimp, peeled and deveined
- 1 cup flour
- 2 eggs, beaten
- Vegetable oil

Lightly toast the coconut on a cookie sheet in a 350 degrees F oven for 8 to 10 minutes.

Butterfly each shrimp by splitting lengthwise down the center, cutting three-fourths of the way through. Dredge the shrimp in flour and then dip in egg. Press the shredded coconut into the shrimp and then fry in 350 degrees F vegetable oil until golden brown.

Serve with Jalapeño Jelly.

Jalapeño Jelly

- 1 cup red wine vinegar
- 1 cup water
- 1 cup granulated sugar
- 2 green jalapeño peppers, seeded and minced

- 1 small red bell pepper, minced
- 1 package liquid pectin

Place all ingredients, except pectin, in a saucepan and bring to a boil. Add the pectin and bring to a boil again. Remove from heat and cool.

The Jalapeño Jelly can be stored in an airtight container in the refrigerator for 7 to 14 days.

Coconut Tempura Shrimp

- 2/3 cup flour
- 1/2 cup cornstarch
- 1 large egg, beaten
- 1 cup grated fresh coconut
- 1 cup ice-cold soda water
- Salt
- 1 pound large shrimp, peeled, deveined, and tail on
- Creole seasoning
- 1 jar mango chutney
- 1 plantain
- 1 tablespoon cilantro, finely chopped

Preheat the fryer.

In a medium-size mixing bowl, combine the flour, cornstarch, egg, coconut, and soda water. Mix well to make a smooth batter. Season with salt. Season the shrimp with Creole seasoning. Holding the tail of the shrimp, dip in the batter, coating completely and shaking off the excess. Fry the shrimp in batches until golden brown, about 4 to 6 minutes. Remove and drain on paper towels. Season with Creole seasoning.

Peel the plantains. Slice the plantains thinly, lengthwise. Fry them until golden brown. Remove and drain on paper towels. Season with Creole seasoning.

Mound some mango chutney in the center of each plate. Lay the shrimp around the chutney. Garnish with fried plantains and cilantro.

Cornsicles with Shrimp and Oregano

- 6 ears corn
- 1 teaspoon salt
- 1/4 teaspoon white pepper
- 1 tablespoon chopped fresh Mexican oregano or
- 1 teaspoon dried Mexican oregano
- 12 medium shrimp
- 24 Popsicle sticks

Peel, devein and dice shrimp. Trim the corn and remove the husks and silk. Save and wash the larger husks. Cut the corn kernels from the cob, scraping out as much milk as you can. Grind the kernels using a meat grinder with a sharp blade. Add the salt, white pepper, oregano and shrimp. Mix well.

Preheat oven to 325 degrees F.

Drop a tablespoon of the corn mixture onto the center of a clean husk. Fold the left side of the husk into the center, then the right, and then fold the bottom end upward. Push a Popsicle stick 2 to 3 inches into the open end and pinch the husk around the stick with your fingers. Tear a thin strand from a dry husk and tie it around the cornsicle. Place the rolls, sticks in the air and very close together, in a glass baking dish or loaf pan. Bake 30 minutes, until the corn mixture is firm and solid.

To eat a cornsicle, peel off the corn husk and eat it hot from the stick, as you would a Popsicle.

Creamy Pesto Shrimp

- 1 pound linguine pasta
- 1/2 cup butter
- 2 cups heavy cream
- 1/2 teaspoon ground black pepper
- 1 cup grated Parmesan cheese
- 1/3 cup pesto (recipe follows)
- 1 pound large shrimp, peeled and deveined

Bring a large pot of lightly salted water to a boil. Add linguine pasta, and cook for 8 to 10 minutes, or until al dente; drain. In a large skillet, melt

the butter over medium heat. Stir in cream, and season with pepper. Cook 6 to 8 minutes, stirring constantly. Stir Parmesan cheese into cream sauce, stirring until thoroughly mixed. Blend in the pesto, and cook for 3 to 5 minutes, until thickened. Stir in the shrimp, and cook until they turn pink, about 5 minutes. Serve over the hot linguine.

Pesto Sauce:

- 1 1/2 cups packed tender young basil leaves
- 2 heaping tablespoons pine nuts
- 1 teaspoon coarse salt

- 1/4 cup extra-virgin olive oil or more to taste 2 garlic cloves, very finely minced
- 1/4 cup freshly grated Parmigiano cheese

Put the basil, pine nuts, and salt in a food processor or blender and process steadily while you add the oil in a thin but constant stream. The sauce should achieve the consistency of a slightly grainy paste but not a fine puree. Add the garlic and process very briefly, just to mix. When the sauce is the right consistency, transfer it to a bowl and, using a spatula, fold in the grated cheese. (If you're using a mortar, just continue to work in the cheese with the pestle.) If the sauce is too thick, work in more olive oil. Taste and adjust the seasoning.

Delta Shrimp

- 2 quarts water
- 1/2 large lemon, sliced
- 2 1/2 pounds unpeeled large fresh shrimp
- 1 cup vegetable oil
- 2 tablespoons hot sauce
- 1 1/2 teaspoons olive oil
- 1 1/2 teaspoons minced garlic
- 1 teaspoon minced fresh parsley
- 3/4 teaspoon salt
- 3/4 teaspoon Old Bay® seasoning
- 3/4 teaspoon dried whole basil
- 3/4 teaspoon dried whole oregano
- 3/4 teaspoon dried whole thyme
- Leaf lettuce

Bring water and lemon to a boil; add shrimp and cook 3 to 5 minutes. Drain well; rinse with cold water. Peel and devein shrimp, leaving tails intact. Place shrimp in a large bowl.

Combine oil and next 9 ingredients; stir with a wire whisk. Pour over shrimp. Toss to coat shrimp.

Easy Creamed Shrimp

- 3 cans cream of shrimp soup
- 1 1/2 teaspoons curry powder
- 3 cups sour cream
- 1 1/2 pounds shrimp, cooked and peeled

Combine all ingredients and heat in top of double boiler.

Serve over rice or in patty shells.

Eggplant Canoes

- 4 medium eggplants
- 1 cup onions, chopped
- 1 cup green onions, chopped
- 4 cloves garlic, chopped
- 1 cup bell pepper, chopped
- 1/2 cup celery, chopped
- 2 bay leaves
- 1 teaspoon thyme
- 4 teaspoons salt
- 1 teaspoon black pepper
- 4 tablespoons bacon grease
- 1 1/2 pounds raw shrimp, peeled
- 1/2 cup (1 stick) butter
- 1 tablespoon Worcestershire sauce
- 1 teaspoon Louisiana hot sauce
- 1 cup seasoned Italian bread crumbs
- 2 eggs, beaten
- 1/2 cup parsley, chopped
- 1 pound lump crabmeat
- 3 tablespoons lemon juice
- 8 tablespoons Romano cheese, grated
- 1 cup sharp Cheddar cheese, grated

Cut eggplants in half lengthwise and boil in salted water for about 10 minutes or until tender. Scoop out insides and chop finely. Place eggplant shells in a shallow baking dish. Sauté onions, green onions, garlic, bell pepper, celery, bay leaves, thyme, salt and pepper in bacon grease for about 15 to 20 minutes. Add chopped eggplant and cook covered for about 30 minutes.

In a separate skillet, sauté shrimp in butter until they turn pink, about 2 minutes, then add to eggplant mixture. Add Worcestershire sauce, hot sauce, bread crumbs and eggs to eggplant mixture. Stir in parsley and lemon juice. Add cheese. Gently fold in crabmeat. Fill eggplant shells with mixture. Bake uncovered at 350 degrees F until hot and browned, about 30 minutes.

Yields 8 servings

Fernandina Shrimp Gravy

- 1 tablespoon granulated sugar
- 1 tablespoon plus 1 cup water
- 2 ounces salt pork, diced
- 1/2 cup minced onion
- 1/2 cup diced green bell pepper
- 1/2 cup diced red bell pepper
- 1/2 cup diced celery
- 1 1/2 pounds shrimp, shelled, cleaned and, if large, cut into pieces
- 1 teaspoon salt
- 1/4 teaspoon freshly-ground black pepper
- 1/8 teaspoon crushed dried red pepper
- 2 cups hot cooked rice

In a heavy, medium-size skillet, stir the sugar over moderate heat until it begins to melt. Continue to cook until the syrup turns golden. Add the tablespoon of water, protecting your hands with a pot holder as the hot sugar may spatter. Stir until the sugar is dissolved. Set this caramel aside.

In a large skillet or sauté pan, cook the salt pork until browned, stirring now and then. Remove the pork bits with a slotted spoon, and set aside. Pour off all but 1 tablespoon of pork drippings. Add the onion, green and red peppers and celery. Sauté until the vegetables are tender. Add the shrimp and cook until they turn bright pink and are opaque, 2 to 3 minutes. Remove the shrimp and vegetables with a slotted spoon and keep them warm on a plate. Add the remaining 1 cup water and 1 teaspoon of the caramel to the pan drippings. Bring to a boil, stir, and simmer 1 to 2 minutes. Season with salt, black pepper and crushed red pepper. Return the shrimp and vegetables and the salt pork bits to the gravy and heat a minute or two.

Serve hot over rice.

Fried Breaded Shrimp

1/4 cup flour
Salt and pepper
1egg
2tablespoons vodka
3/4 cup fine bread crumbs
40 large raw shrimp, shelled, but with tails intact
Oil (for frying)

Mix flour with a little salt and pepper and place in a bowl. In a second bowl beat well the egg and vodka. In a third bowl place the bread crumbs mixed with salt and pepper. Toss the shrimp, one at a time, in the flour; dip into egg mixture; toss in the bread crumbs to coat. Drop into hot oil (360 degrees

and deep fry quickly until golden brown. Do not overcook. Shrimp may be breaded several hours ahead and refrigerated until time to fry. Serve with a tartar and a cocktail sauce.

Serves 3 to 4.

Gambas al Ajillo (Garlic Shrimp)

- 2 tablespoons olive oil
- 4 cloves garlic, sliced thinly
- 1 tablespoon crushed red pepper (or 3 guindilla peppers, crushed)
- 1 pound shrimp
- salt and pepper, to taste

Heat the olive oil in a skillet on medium heat. Add the garlic and red pepper. Saute until the garlic is browned, stirring often to make sure the garlic doesn't burn.

Toss the shrimp in the oil (be careful that the oil doesn't splash up on you). Cook for 2 minutes on each side, until pink.
Add the salt and pepper. Cook for another minute before removing from the heat. Serve with slices of baguette (tapas-style) or with pasta.

If you're tossing with pasta:

Start in a large saucepan. Cook shrimp as instructed, while making pasta in a separate pot (you will probably start the pasta before the shrimp, since the shrimp only takes 5-7 minutes) . While draining the pasta, reserve some of the pasta water. When the shrimp is finished, pour the cooked pasta into the saucepan with the shrimp and toss well, coating the pasta with the garlic and red pepper-infused oil. Add reserved pasta water, in tablespoon increments, if necessary. Top with chopped parsley.

Grilled Marinated Shrimp

Ingredients

1 cup olive oil
1/4 cup chopped fresh parsley
1 lemon, juiced
2 tablespoons hot pepper sauce
3 cloves garlic, minced
1 tablespoon tomato paste
2 teaspoons dried oregano
1 teaspoon salt
1 teaspoon ground black pepper
2 pounds large shrimp, peeled and deveined with
tails attached
Skewers

Directions

In a mixing bowl, mix together olive oil, parsley,
lemon juice, hot sauce, garlic, tomato paste,
oregano, salt, and black pepper. Reserve a small
amount for basting later. Pour remaining marinade
into a large resealable plastic bag with shrimp.
Seal, and marinate in the refrigerator for 2 hours.

Preheat grill for medium-low heat. Thread shrimp onto skewers, piercing once near the tail and once near the head. Discard marinade.

Lightly oil grill grate. Cook shrimp for 5 minutes per side, or until opaque, basting frequently with reserved marinade.

Texas Shrimp

- 1/4 cup vegetable oil
- 1/4 cup tequila
- 1/4 cup red wine vinegar
- 2 tablespoons Mexican lime juice
- 1 tablespoon ground red chiles
- 1/2 teaspoon salt
- 2 cloves garlic, finely chopped
- 1 red bell pepper, finely chopped
- 24 large raw shrimp, peeled and de-veined (tails left on)

Mix all ingredients except shrimp in shallow glass or plastic dish. Stir in shrimp. Cover and refrigerate for 1 hour.

Remove shrimp from marinade, reserving marinade. Thread 4 shrimp on each of six (8-inch) metal skewers. Grill over medium coals, turning once, until pink, 2 to 3 minutes on each side.

Heat marinade to boiling in a nonreactive saucepan. Reduce heat to low. Simmer uncovered until bell pepper is tender, about 5 minutes. Serve with shrimp.

Makes 6 servings

NOTE: If you would prefer to broil the shrimp instead of grilling them, place the skewered shrimp on a broiler pan rack. Broil with tops about 4 inches from heat, turning once, until pink, 2 to 3 minutes on each side.

Hawaiian shrimp Skewers

- 1/2 pound shrimp, peeled, deveined & uncooked 1/2 pound bay or sea scallops 1 can pineapple chunks in juice
- 1 green bell pepper, cut in wedges
- bacon slices

Sauce:

- 6 ounces barbecue sauce
- 16 ounces salsa
- 2 tablespoons pineapple juice
- 2 tablespoons white wine

Blend sauce ingredients until evenly mixed. Skewer pineapple chunks, shrimp, scallops, bell pepper wedges, and bacon slices folded. Baste skewer evenly on each side and grill. Cook until shrimp are a pink color. Serve with rice.

Honey-Thyme Grilled Shrimp

Roasted Garlic Marinade

2 pounds fresh or frozen uncooked large shrimp in shells

1 medium red bell pepper, cut into 1-inch squares and blanched

1 medium yellow bell pepper, cut into 1-inch squares and blanched

1 medium red onion, cut into quarters and separated into chunks

Prepare Roasted Garlic Marinade (recipe follows).

Peel shrimp. (If shrimp are frozen, do not thaw; peel in cold water.) Make a shallow cut lengthwise down back of each shrimp; wash out vein.

Pour 1/2 cup of the marinade into small resealable plastic bag; seal bag and refrigerate until serving. Pour remaining marinade into large resealable plastic bag. Add shrimp, bell peppers and onion, turning to coat with marinade. Seal bag and refrigerate at least 2 hours but no longer than 24 hours.

Brush grill rack with vegetable oil. Heat coals or gas grill for direct heat. Remove shrimp and vegetables from marinade; drain well. Discard marinade. Thread shrimp and vegetables alternately on each of six 15-inch metal skewers, leaving space between each.

Grill kabobs uncovered 4 to 6 inches from HOT heat 7 to 10 minutes, turning once, until shrimp are pink and firm. Place kabobs on serving tray. Cut a tiny corner from small plastic bag of reserved marinade, using scissors. Drizzle marinade over shrimp and vegetables.

Yield: 6 servings.

Roasted Garlic Marinade

1 medium bulb garlic

1/3 cup olive or vegetable oil

2/3 cup orange juice

1/4 cup spicy honey mustard

3 tablespoons honey

3/4 teaspoon dried thyme leaves, crushed

Preheat oven to 375 degrees F. Cut one-third off top of unpeeled garlic bulb, exposing cloves. Place garlic in small baking dish; drizzle with oil. Cover tightly and bake 45 minutes; cool. Squeeze garlic pulp from papery skin. Place garlic and remaining ingredients in blender. Cover and blend on high speed until smooth. Makes about 1 1/2 cups.

Hot and Spicy Shrimp

1 pound butter

1/4 cup peanut oil

3 cloves garlic, chopped

2 tablespoons rosemary

1 teaspoon chopped basil

1 teaspoon chopped thyme

1 teaspoon chopped oregano

1 small hot pepper, chopped, or

2 tablespoons ground cayenne pepper

2 teaspoons fresh ground black pepper

2 bay leaves, crumbled

1 tablespoon paprika

2 teaspoons lemon juice

2 pounds raw shrimp in their shells

Salt

Shrimp should be of a size to number 30–35 per pound.

Melt the butter and oil in a flameproof baking dish. Add the garlic, herbs, peppers, bay leaves, paprika, and lemon juice, and bring to a boil. Turn the heat down and simmer 10 minutes, stirring frequently. Remove the dish from the heat and let the flavors marry at least 30 minutes.

This hot butter sauce can be made a day in advance and refrigerated. Preheat the oven to 450 degrees F. Reheat the sauce, add the shrimp, and cook over medium heat until the shrimp just turn pink, then bake in the oven about 30 minutes more. Taste for seasoning, adding salt if necessary. Sop up butter sauce with crusty bread after the shrimp have been eaten.

Italian Broiled Shrimp

2 pounds jumbo shrimp

1/4 cup olive oil

2 tablespoons garlic, minced

1/4 cup flour

1/4 cup butter, melted

4 tablespoons parsley, minced

1 cup Drawn Butter Sauce

Shell shrimp, leaving tails on. Dry, then dust with flour. Stir oil and butter into flat baking dish; add shrimp. Broil at medium heat for 8 minutes. Add garlic and parsley to Drawn Butter Sauce. Pour over shrimp. Stir until shrimp are coated. Broil 2 more minutes.

Jerk Shrimp with Sweet Jamaican Rice

1 pound medium shrimp (51–60 count), raw, shell on
Jerk seasoning

2 cups hot cooked rice

1 (11 ounce) can mandarin oranges, drained and chopped

1 (8 ounce) can crushed pineapple, drained

1/2 cup chopped red bell pepper

1/4 cup slivered almonds, toasted

1/2 cup sliced scallions

2 tablespoons flaked coconut, toasted

1/4 teaspoon ground ginger

Prepare jerk marinade according to package instructions on back of jerk seasoning.

Peel and devein shrimp leaving the tail on. Place in marinade while preparing rice.

In large skillet, combine all remaining ingredients. Cook over medium-high heat, stirring constantly for 5 minutes or until thoroughly heated. Remove shrimp from marinade. Place in broiler pan in single layer. Broil 5 to 6 inches from heat for 2 minutes.

Stir well and broil an additional 2 minutes or until shrimp are just pink.

Serve with rice.

Killer Shrimp

2 tablespoons dried rosemary

2 teaspoons dried thyme

1/2 teaspoon fennel seed

1 teaspoon black pepper

5 cloves garlic, peeled and chopped

1 teaspoon celery seed

1 teaspoon crushed red pepper flakes

2 quarts low-sodium chicken broth

8 ounces clam juice

3 ounces tomato paste

1/2 cup (1 stick) butter

1 cup white wine

1 1/2 pounds raw peeled shrimp, with tails

French bread (for dipping)

Partially break up the rosemary, thyme, and fennel seed with fingers or mortar and pestle.

Place all ingredients, except wine and shrimp, in a large pot. Simmer for about 30 minutes, then add wine. Continue to simmer for a total cooking time of no more than 2 hours.

Just before serving, add raw shrimp. Simmer until shrimp is done, stirring, about 2 minutes.

Each bowl should contain a serving of shrimp and a lot of broth, which should almost completely cover the shrimp. The dish is eaten with your fingers. Soak up the broth with the bread.

Yields 4 servings.

Lemon-Garlic Broiled Shrimp

2 pounds medium shrimp, peeled and deveined
2 cloves garlic, halved
1/4 cup butter or margarine, melted
1/2 teaspoon salt
Coarse ground pepper
3 drops hot sauce
1 tablespoon Worcestershire sauce
5 tablespoons chopped fresh parsley

Place shrimp in single layer in a 15 x 10 x 1-inch
jellyroll pan; set aside.
Sauté garlic in butter until garlic is browned;
remove and discard garlic. Add remaining
ingredients, except parsley, stirring well. Pour
mixture over shrimp. Broil shrimp4 inches from
heat for 8 to 10 minutes, basting once. Sprinkle
with parsley.
Yields 6 servings.

Lime Pepper Shrimp

1 pound large shrimp, peeled and deveined
1 tablespoon olive oil
1 Tablespoon minced fresh rosemary
1 tablespoon minced fresh thyme
2 teaspoons minced garlic
1 teaspoon coarsely-ground black pepper
Pinch of ground red pepper
Juice of one lime

In a medium bowl, combine the shrimp, oil, herbs and peppers. Mix well to coat the shrimp. Let stand at room temperature for 20 minutes.

Heat a large no-stick frying pan over medium-high heat for 3 minutes. Add the shrimp in a single layer. Cook for 3 minutes per side, or until the shrimp a pink and just cooked through. Do not overcook. Remove from heat and stir in lime juice.

Louisiana Shrimp Esplanade

24 large fresh shrimp
12 ounces butter
1 tablespoon puréed garlic
2 tablespoons Worcestershire sauce
1 teaspoon dried thyme
1 teaspoon dried rosemary
1/2 teaspoon dried oregano
1/2 teaspoon crushed red pepper
1 teaspoon cayenne pepper
1 teaspoon black pepper
8 ounces beer
4 cups cooked white rice
1/2 cup finely chopped scallions

Wash shrimp and leave in the shell. Melt butter in
a large frying pan and stir in the garlic,
Worcestershire sauce and seasonings.
Add shrimp and shake the pan to immerse the
shrimp in butter, then sauté over medium–high
heat for 4 to 5 minutes until they turn pink.
Next, pour in the beer and stir for a further
minute, then remove from the heat. Shell and
devein the shrimp and arrange on a bed of rice.
Pour the pan juices on top and garnish with
chopped scallion.

Serve immediately.

Malibu Stir Fry Shrimp

1 tablespoon peanut oil
1 tablespoon butter
1 tablespoon minced garlic
1 pound medium shrimp, shelled and deveined
1 cup sliced mushrooms
1 bunch scallions, sliced
1 red sweet pepper, seeded, cut in thin 2" strips
1 cup fresh or frozen peas
1 cup Malibu rum
1 cup heavy cream
1/4 cup chopped fresh basil or 1 tablespoon dried
2 teaspoons ground chili paste or 2 tablespoons prepared chili sauce
Juice of 1/2 lime
Fresh ground black pepper
1/2 cup shredded coconut
1 pound fettuccini, cooked

Heat oil and butter over high heat in large pan. Add garlic for 1 minute. Add shrimp, cook 2 minutes until pink. Add vegetables and fry 2 minutes. Add rum and simmer 2 minutes. Add cream and simmer 5 minutes. Add remaining seasonings. Toss with coconut and cooked pasta.

Outa Sight Shrimp

4 pounds unpeeled, large fresh shrimp or 6 pound
shrimp with heads on
1/2 cup butter
1/2 cup olive oil
1/4 cup chili sauce
1/4 cup Worcestershire sauce
2 lemons, sliced
4 garlic cloves, chopped
2 tablespoons Creole seasoning
2 tablespoons lemon juice
1 tablespoon chopped parsley
1 teaspoon paprika
1 teaspoon oregano
1 teaspoon ground red pepper
1/2 teaspoon hot sauce
French bread
Spread shrimp in a shallow, aluminum foil-lined
broiler pan. Combine butter and next 12
ingredients in a saucepan over low heat, stirring
until butter melts, and pour over shrimp. Cover and
chill 2 hours, turning shrimp every 30 minutes.

Bake, uncovered, at 400 degrees F for 20 minutes;
turn once.

Serve with bread, green salad and corn on the cob
for a complete meal.

Really Cool Shrimp Salad

2 Lbs. Medium Shrimp

1 Cup Miracle Whip

1/2 Cup Green Onions

1 Green Bell Pepper

1 Small Head of Lettuce

1 Medium Tomato

1/2 Cup Mozzarella Cheese

Peel, devein, and boil shrimp. Chop lettuce, bell pepper, tomato, green onions and shrimp, and mix together in bowl... Shred mozzarella cheese and add to salad.. Add miracle whip and mix together well. Refrigerate for at least one hour and serve by itself or with your favorite seafood meal.....

M-80 Rock Shrimp

M-80 Sauce

- 1 tablespoon cornstarch
- 1 cup water
- 1 cup soy sauce
- 1 cup light brown sugar
- 1 tablespoon sambal chile paste
- cup freshly squeezed orange juice 1 serrano chile, finely chopped
- cloves garlic, finely chopped (about 1 tablespoon)
- One two-inch piece fresh ginger, scraped/peeled and finely chopped

Slaw

- head green cabbage, thinly sliced (about $1\frac{1}{2}$ cups)
- head red cabbage, thinly sliced (about $1\frac{1}{2}$ cups)
- medium carrot, thinly sliced into 2-inch pieces
- medium red pepper, thinly sliced
- medium red onion, thinly sliced
- 1 garlic clove, thinly sliced
- 1 Serrano chile, thinly sliced

- basil leaves, thinly sliced

Shrimp

- Vegetable oil
- 2 pound rock shrimp (or substitute 16-20 count shrimp cut into small cubes) 1 cup buttermilk
- 3 cup all-purpose flour
- Black and white sesame seeds
- 1 tablespoon green onions, thinly sliced
- Cilantro leaves

Make the M-80 sauce: In a small bowl, whisk together the cornstarch and water. Set aside. In a small saucepan, whisk together the soy sauce, brown sugar, chile paste, orange juice, chile, garlic and ginger and bring the sauce to a boil. Lower the heat and simmer for 15 minutes. Whisk in the cornstarch-water mixture and bring the sauce back up to a boil.

Make the slaw: In a medium bowl, toss together the green and red cabbage, carrot, red pepper, onion, garlic, chile and basil. Set aside.

Make the shrimp: In a medium saucepan set over high heat, add enough oil to come halfway up the pot; heat until the oil reaches 350° (use a thermometer to measure the temperature). Put the rock shrimp in a large bowl and pour the buttermilk over them. Use a slotted spoon to remove the shrimp, drain off the excess buttermilk and, in a separate bowl, toss the shrimp with the flour. Fry the shrimp for 1 to $1\frac{1}{2}$ Minutes.

Toast of the Town

INGREDIENTS

Twelve 16-20 count shrimp, deveined and shells removed

Salt and freshly ground black pepper

avocados

tablespoons lime juice (about 1 medium lime), divided

tablespoons finely chopped cilantro

teaspoons finely chopped jalapeño (about 1 medium jalapeño)

1 grapefruit

1 small baguette, sliced into $\frac{1}{4}$-inch slices Extra-virgin olive oil

Salt and freshly ground black pepper $\frac{1}{4}$ cup pistachios, toasted and chopped

DIRECTIONS

Place the shrimp on a small plate and season with salt and pepper. Cut the avocados lengthwise around the pits and remove the pits. Cut the avocado flesh in a crosshatch pattern and use a spoon to scoop the avocado flesh into a medium bowl. Combine the avocado with $1\frac{1}{2}$ tablespoons of the lime juice and the cilantro and jalapeño.

Use a knife to remove the skin and any pith from the grapefruit flesh and slice along the membranes to remove the segments. Set aside.

Brush the baguette slices with olive oil and season with salt and pepper. Place the baguette slices in the toaster and toast until golden brown.

In a medium skillet set over medium heat, heat $1\frac{1}{2}$ tablespoons of olive oil and add the shrimp. Cook for one minute on one side, then flip and cook an additional 30 seconds on the other side. Transfer the shrimp to a bowl and toss with the remaining $\frac{1}{2}$ tablespoon of lime juice.

To assemble: Spread 2 tablespoons of avocado mixture on each baguette slice. Top with one or two pieces of shrimp and a segment of grapefruit. Sprinkle pistachios over the top and serve immediately.

Shrimp Curry with Mustard

The unique combination of shrimps and mustard is a culinary delight.

Ingredients:

- 1 lb. shrimps
- 2 tbsp. oil
- 1 tsp. turmeric
- 2 tbsp. mustard powder
- 1 tsp. salt
- 8 green chillies

Method:

Make a paste of mustard in an equal amount of water. Heat oil in a non-stick frying pan and fry the mustard paste and the shrimps for at least five minutes, and add 2 cups of lukewarm water.

Bring to a boil and add turmeric and salt and green chillies. Cook on medium low heat foranother twenty five minutes.

Shrimp Curry

Ingredients:

- 1 lb. shrimps, peeled and deveined
- 1 onion, pureed
- 1 tsp. ginger paste
- 1 tsp. garlic paste
- 1 tomato, pureed
- 1 tsp. turmeric powder
- 1 tsp. chilli powder
- 1 tsp. cumin powder
- 1 tsp. coriander powder
- 1 tsp. salt or to taste
- 1 tsp. lemon juice
- Cilantro/coriander leaves
- 1 tbsp. oil

Method:

Heat oil in a non-stick frying pan and fry the onion, tomato, ginger and garlic, together with cumin and coriander powders and cilantro/coriander leaves for five minutes on medium low heat. Add shrimp, turmeric and chili powders and salt together with half a cup of lukewarm water and cook on medium low heat for twenty five minutes. Keep the pan covered with a lid. Stir well to let the shrimps blend with the spices. Season with lemon juice, garnish with cilantro/coriander before serving.

Note: Using pre-cooked, peeled and deveined shrimp available in the grocery store to reduce preparation time.

Shrimp in Garlic Sauce

12 cloves garlic, roughly chopped

1 cup vegetable oil

1/4 cup (1/2 stick) unsalted butter

1 1/2 pounds fresh shrimp, peeled, de-veinedand butterflied (leave tails intact)

In a large skillet, sauté the garlic in medium-hot oil (about 300 degrees F) until light brown. Watch carefully so as not to burn. After about 6 to 8 minutes, quickly whisk in the butter and remove immediately from the fire. When all the butter has been added, the bits will become crisp. Remove them with a slotted spoon and reserve the oil and butter for sautéing the shrimp.

In a large skillet, heat about 2 to 3 tablespoons of the reserved oil and then sauté the shrimp for about 5 minutes. Turn over very briefly and then remove. Add more oil as necessary to sauté all the shrimp. Salt to taste. Garnish with garlic bits and parsley. Serve with Mexican Rice.

Try brushing garlic oil over French bread, then sprinkling it with parsley and toasting it.

Serve this with the shrimp and accompany the dish with a lettuce and tomato salad.

Shrimp in Mustard Cream Sauce

1 pound large shrimp

2 tablespoons vegetable oil

1 shallot, minced

3 tablespoons dry white wine

1/2 cup heavy cream or whipping cream

1 tablespoon Dijon mustard with seed

Salt, to taste

Shell and devein shrimp. In a 10-inch skillet over medium heat cook shallot in hot oil for 5 minutes, stirring often. Increase heat to medium-high. Add shrimp. Cook 5 minutes or until shrimp turns pink, stirring often. Remove shrimp to bowl. Add wine to drippings in skillet. Cook over medium heat for 2 minutes. Add cream and mustard. Cook for 2 minutes. Return shrimp to skillet. Stir until heated through. Salt to taste.

Serve over hot, cooked rice.

Serves 4.

Gazpacho

Ingredients

- 2 cloves garlic
- 1/2 red onion
- 5 Roma tomatoes
- 2 stalks celery
- 1 large cucumber
- 1 zucchini
- 1/4 cup extra-virgin olive oil
- 2 tablespoons red wine vinegar
- 2 tablespoons sugar Several dashes hot sauce Dash salt
- Dash black pepper
- 4 cups good-quality tomato juice
- 1 pound shrimp, peeled and deveined Avocado slices, for serving
- hard-boiled eggs, finely minced Fresh cilantro leaves, for serving Crusty bread, for serving

Directions

Mince up the garlic, cut the onion into slices, and dice up the tomatoes, celery, cucumber and zucchini. Throw all the garlic, all the onion, half of the remaining diced vegetables and the oil into the bowl of a food processor or, if you like, a blender.

Splash in the vinegar and add the sugar, hot sauce, salt and pepper. Finally pour in 2 cups of the tomato juice and blend well. You'll basically have a tomato base with a beautiful confetti of vegetables.

Pour the blended mixture into a large bowl and add in the other half of the diced vegetables. Stir it together. Then stir in the remaining 2 cups tomato juice. Give it a taste and make sure the seasoning is right. Adjust as needed. Refrigerate for an hour if possible.

Grill or saute the shrimp until opaque. Set aside. Ladle the soup into bowls, add the grilled shrimp and garnish with avocado slices, egg and cilantro leaves. Serve with crusty bread on the side.

Shrimp Linguine Alfredo

1 (12 ounce) package linguine pasta

1/4 cup butter, melted

4 tablespoons diced onion

4 teaspoons minced garlic

40 small shrimp, peeled and deveined

1 cup half-and-half

2 teaspoons ground black pepper

6 tablespoons grated Parmesan cheese

4 sprigs fresh parsley

4 slices lemon, for garnish

Cook pasta in a large pot of boiling water until al dente; drain. Meanwhile, melt butter in a large saucepan. Saute onion and garlic over medium heat until tender. Add shrimp; saute over high heat for 1 minute, stirring constantly. Stir in half-and-half. Cook, stirring constantly, until sauce thickens. Place pasta in a serving dish, and cover with shrimp sauce. Sprinkle with black pepper and Parmesan cheese. Garnish with parsley and lemon slices.

Shrimp Marinara

1 (16 oz.) can of tomatoes, cut up

2 tbsp. minced parsley

1 clove garlic, minced

1/2 tsp. dried basil

1 tsp. salt

1/4 tsp. pepper

1 tsp. dried oregano

1 (6 oz.) can tomato paste

1/2 tsp. seasoned salt

1 lb. cooked shelled shrimp

Grated Parmesan cheese

Cooked spaghetti

In a crock pot, combine tomatoes with parsley, garlic, basil, salt, pepper, oregano, tomato paste, and seasoned salt. Cover and cook on low for 6 to 7 hours.

Turn control to high, stir in shrimp, cover and cook on high for 10 to 15 minutes more. Serve over cooked spaghetti.

Top with Parmesan cheese.

Shrimp Newburg

1 pound shrimp, cooked, deveined

1 (4 ounce can mushrooms

3 hard-boiled eggs, peeled and chopped

1/2 cup Parmesan cheese

4 tablespoons butter

1/2 onion, chopped

1 clove garlic, chopped

6 tablespoons flour

3 cups milk

4 tablespoons dry sherry

Worcestershire sauce

Salt and pepper

Tabasco sauce

Preheat oven to 375 degrees F.

Melt butter and then sauté the onion and garlic until tender. Add the flour. Mix well. Gradually add the milk, stirring constantly. Cook until the sauce thickens. Add the sherry and the seasonings to taste.

In a separate bowl, combine shrimp, mushrooms, eggs, and parsley. Add sauce along with 1/4 cup cheese to shrimp mixture. Mix well.

Pour the mixture into a 2-quart casserole dish and top with remaining cheese. Dot with the butter.

Bake 10 minutes, until slightly browned on top.

Spicy Marinated Shrimp

2 lbs. Large shrimp, peeled and deveined

1 Teaspoon Salt

1 Lemon, cut in half

8 Cup Water

Cup White wine vinegar or tarragon vinegar

Cup Olive oil

1–2 Serrano chiles (more or less, depending on taste), seeds and veins removed, finely minced

$\frac{1}{4}$ Cup Fresh cilantro, chopped

2 Large cloves garlic, minced or put through a garlic press

2 Teaspoon Fresh cilantro, chopped (if desired)

3 Green onions (white part only), minced

Freshly ground black pepper, to taste

Combine the water, salt and lemon halves in a Dutch oven, and bring to a boil. Add the shrimp, stir, and boil gently for 4–5 minutes. Remove from heat and drain.

Combine the vinegar, olive oil, chiles, cilantro and garlic in a large zip-top plastic bag or other plastic container. Add the boiled shrimp, and refrigerate for 12 hours or overnight, turning several times.

To serve, drain liquid from shrimp. In a large bowl, combine chilled shrimp with additional cilantro, green onions and black pepper, and toss well. Arrange in a serving dish, and serve immediately.

Spicy Singapore Shrimp

2 pounds large shrimp (Parr recommends head-on shrimp)

2 tablespoons ketchup

3 tablespoons Sriracha

2 tablespoons lemon juice

2 tablespoons soy sauce

1 tablespoon sugar

2 medium jalapeños, seeded and minced

white bulb of 1 stalk of lemongrass, minced

1 tablespoon fresh ginger, minced

4 scallions, sliced thinly

1/4 cup cilantro, chopped

Combine the ketchup, vinegar (if using), chili sauce, lemon juice, soy sauce and sugar.

In a large skillet, heat up a little vegetable oil and cook the shrimp on high heat. When they start to turn pink, flip them.
Add a little bit more oil and the jalapeños, garlic, lemongrass and ginger. Stir often until the mixture is heated through. Warning: it will smell delicious. Try not to lose your focus.

Stir-fry the scallions and the ketchup mixture in the skillet for 30 seconds, then mix in the chopped cilantro. Serve the shrimp with rice.

Starlight Shrimp

- 6 cups of water
- 2 tbsp. salt
- 1 lemon, halved
- 1 stalk celery, cut into 3 inch pieces
- 2 bay leaves
- A dash of cayenne pepper
- 1/4 cup parsley, minced
- 1 package Zatarains Crawfish/Crab/Shrimp boil (if available)
- 2 lbs. unpeeled shrimp freshly trolled in Mobile Bay
- 1 container of cocktail sauce

Slice off heads of shrimp.

Combine first 8 ingredients in a large pot or Dutch Oven. Bring to boil. Add shrimp in shells and cook about 5 minutes until they become pink. Drain well with cold water and chill.

Peel and devein shrimp, then store in chilled cooler.

Zesty Alabama Cocktail Sauce

- 2/3 cup chili sauce
- 1/4 cup lemon juice
- 2 to 3 tbsp. prepared horseradish
- 2 tsp. Worcestershire sauce
- 1/4 tsp. hot sauce

Mix all ingredients together. Sample and add to your taste. The more, the zestier! Store in chilled cooler.

Carry the cooler to the beach and, as the sun fades over the Gulf waters and Jimmy Buffett's rendition of "Stars Fell On Alabama" plays softly in the background, enjoy the shrimp, perhaps with a glass of wine or beer.

Butterfly Shrimp

- 1 lb. extra-large shrimp
- 4 slices bacon
- 1 large onion
- 1 garlic clove
- 2 eggs
- 4 Tbsp. flour
- 2 cups vegetable oil

For sauce:

- 1/4 cup catsup
- 2 Tbsp. Worcestershire sauce
- 3 Tbsp. sugar
- Dash pepper
- 1/2 cup water
- 2 Tbsp. cornstarch
- 2 Tbsp. water
- 1 Tbsp. oil
- 1/2 tsp. salt

Shell, devein and butterfly shrimp. Cut bacon into 1-1/2 inch pieces. Slice onion and saute in oil. Crush garlic. Place slice of bacon over each shrimp. Lay on platter. Beat eggs. Add flour to eggs and beat with wire whisk until batter thickens. Holding shrimp and bacon together dip in batter and place into hot oil for 2-3 minutes. Remove and drain on paper towels. Set aside.

In small bowl mix catsup, Worcestershire sauce, sugar, pepper and water. In a cup blend cornstarch and water. Heat oil and add crushed garlic and salt until golden brown. Add to this the catsup mixture and bring ingredients to a boil. Stir in cornstarch until mixture thickens. Serve shrimp over onions and spoon sauce over shrimp.

Cajun Shrimp

(2 servings)

- 1 lb. shrimp (3-4 inch w/out heads)
- 1/4 tsp. cayenne
- 1 tsp. black pepper
- 1/2 tsp. salt
- 1/2 tsp. red chile pepper flakes
- 1/2 tsp. thyme
- 1/2 tsp. rosemary
- 1/8 tsp. oregano
- 3 Tbsp. butter
- 1 1/2 tsp. garlic, minced
- 1 tsp. Worcestershire sauce
- 1/2 cup beer (room temperature)

Shell, de-vein, and rinse shrimp. Grind seasonings in mortar and pestle. In large skillet over high heat, melt butter; add garlic, seasonings, and Worcestershire sauce. When bubbly, add shrimp. Cook 2 minutes, stirring and shaking the skillet. Add beer and cook 3 minutes. Remove shrimp and reduce sauce, adjusting seasoning. Serve shrimp over rice with sauce spooned over the top.

Chilled Aromatic Shrimp with Cilantro-Ginger-Lime Cream

- 1 cup loosely packed fresh cilantro
- 1 tablespoon fresh ginger, chopped
- 2 cloves garlic
- 2 scallions (green onions), sliced
- 1 jalapeno pepper, halved and seeded
- 1 teaspoon sugar
- One-half teaspoon salt
- 3 tablespoons mild vegetable oil
- 3 tablespoons fresh lime juice
- 1 to 2 pounds medium or large shrimps peeled but with tails left on.
- 1 cup heavy cream

In a food processor, combine cilantro, ginger, garlic, scallions, jalapeno, and process until finely chopped (or chop fine by hand). Add sugar, salt, oil and lime juice and mix well. Toss Shrimp in mixture until well-coated; cover bowl and let stand an hour at cool room temperature or longer in the refrigerator.

Spoon shrimps out of marinade and sauté lightly (without additional oil) until shrimps are barely cooked. Arrange on serving plate and chill.

Add reserved marinade to the liquid from the cooked shrimp and voil, stirring, until the liquid evaporates, leaving a thick green puree. Add cream and boil again, stirring constantly, until thick enough to pour. Do not reduce too much; this sauce thickens considerably as it cools. Pour sauce into a serving bowl and refrigerate with the shrimp until both are well-chilled and ready to serve.

New Orleans BBQ shrimp

- 1 c (2 sticks) margarine
- 1/2 c vegetable oil
- 1/2 c chicken broth (canned is fine)
- 4 t finely minced garlic
- 5 whole bay leaves, torn into pieces
- 4 t dried rosemary, crushed
- 1 t dried sweet basil
- 1 t greek oregano
- 1 t dried thyme
- 1/2 t salt
- 1/2 t (or more) cayenne pepper
- 4 t paprika
- 1 1/2 t freshly ground black pepper
- 1 T fresh lemon juice
- 2 lb whole fresh shrimp in the shell (with heads if possible)

In a heavy sauté pan or saucepan melt the margarine, then add the oil and mix well. Add all the other ingredients except the shrimp and broth, and cook over medium heat, stirring constantly, until the sauce begins to boil. Reduce the heat to low and simmer for 7 to 8 minutes, stirring frequently, then remove the pan from the heat and let it stand, uncovered, at room temperature for at least 30 minutes. Add the shrimp to the sauce, mix thoroughly, and put the pan back on the burner. Cook over medium heat for

6 to 8 minutes or just until the shrimp turn pink. Add the broth, shaking the pan back and forth to mix. Preferably, place the pan into a preheated 450 deg F oven and bake for 10 minutes. OR simmer loosely covered on the stovetop for about 5 or 10 minutes. Serve equal portions of shrimp with about 1/2 c of the sauce ladled over each one. You will need bibs and lots of bread to sop up the sauce. Also, fingers are a necessary eating utensil. A good side dish is quartered red new potatoes, baked in olive oil, lemon juice, salt, pepper, and several bay leaves. A green salad and bread finishes the meal. Makes 5 generous (nearly 1/2 lb) servings

Curried Corn and Shrimp Soup

2 cups regular-strength chicken broth

2 medium-size tart apples (peeled, cored and chopped)

1 large onion (chopped)

1/2 tsp curry powder
1 large red bell pepper (stemmed and seeded)

4 cups cold buttermilk

1/4 cup lime juice

1 1/2 cups cooked corn kernels

1/2 cup minced fresh cilantro

1/3 lb. tiny cooked shrimp

Cilantro Sprigs (optional)

In a 4- to 5- quart pan over high heat combine broth, apples, onion, and curry. Cover and bring to a boil, then simmer until apples mash easily (about

30 min). Let cool, then cover and chill until cold, at least 3 hours or up to a day. Smoothly puree mixture in a blender or food processor.

Cut a few thin slivers from bell pepper and set aside; dice remaining pepper and put into a tureen with apple puree, buttermilk, lime juice, 1 1/4 cups of corn and minced cilantro. Ladle soup into bowls and top with shrimp, remaining corn, bell pepper strips, and cilantro sprigs.

Fiesta Shrimp

- Clean & devein 1 lb shrimp (enough for 2, 4, etc people)

In a wok (on medium to medium high), add:

- 1 TBS butter

When melted, add

- Shrimp
- garlic to taste (I like a lot of garlic so I would put in several cloves chopped finely or put through a garlic press - if you're lazy you can buy jars of minced garlic)

Stir quickly till all shrimp has turned pink Add 1 cup fresh corn (or thawed frozen) Stir quickly to heat through

- Add 1 cup salsa (I prefer hot - choose your own strength)

Stir quickly to heat thoroughly

Serve with Black beans, fresh tossed salad with crumbled blue cheese & warm flour or wheat tortillas

Pasta with Shrimp in Tomato Cream

- 1/3 cup dried tomatoes packed in oil, drained, reserve oil, and slivered. 1 clove garlic, minced or pressed
- 1 lb large (31-35/lb) shrimp, shelled, deveined 1/4 cup thinly sliced green onions, including tops 1 1/2 Tbs chopped fresh basil, or 1 tsp dried basil 1/4 tsp white pepper
- 1 cup chicken broth
- 3/4 cup dry vermouth
- 1 cup whipping cream
- 10 oz linguine
- garnish: grated parmesan cheese and/or fresh basil sprigs

Add 2 Tbs oil from tomatoes, heat in wide frying pan over medium-high heat. Add garlic and shrimp when oil is hot. Cook, while stirring, until shrimp are opaque when cut (about 6 min). Remove from pan. Add onions, chopped basil, tomatoes, pepper, broth vermouth and cream to pan. Boil over high hear, stirring occasionally until reduced to about 1 1/2 cups (about 10 min). Return shrimp to pan and stir until just heated through.

Meanwhile cook linguine in 3 qts boiling water until just al dente (about 8 min for dried linguine).

Drain, arrange on 4 plates and spoon sauce over.
Garnish with basil, cheese to taste.

Caribbean Coconut Shrimp

1 lb shrimp - peeled and deveined

Batter
3/4 cup flour
1 egg
1/2 Tbsp baking powder
1/2 cup beer

Coating
1/4 cup flour
1 1/2 cups dried grated coconut
1 Tbsp salt
1/2 Tbsp ground black pepper
1/2 Tbsp cayenne (or ground chilis)
1/2 Tbsp paprika
1 Tbsp garlic powder(not Garlic salt!)
1/2 tsp dried thyme
1/2 tsp oregano

Dip shrimp individually into the batter and then roll
in the coating.
Deep-fry.
Allow to drain on paper towel.

Serve with various dips: eg. honey + soy sauce +
tobacco; honey + mustard or marmalade + ginger.

Papaya garlic Shrimp

In a saucepan melt 3 Tbsp butter, saute 2 cloves of garlic (chopped, not crushed) and half a cooking onion (actually, spanish onion is better), once the garlic has browned and the onion has cleared, add half a papaya chopped into 1/2 inch chunks and a tsp of dried thyme leaves, stir until papaya just starts to go mushy. Dump all of this into a bowl and then sauté your shrimp in the same saucepan (with a little more butter) for a couple of minutes. Finally, throw the papaya/garlic/onion mixture back in for another 5 min on low heat. Serve over rice or with thai noodles or what have you.

Shrimp Creole

- 2 lbs baby shrimp
- 3 T butter
- 1 C onions, chopped coarsly
- 1 C green pepper, chopped
- 1 C chopped zucchini
- 1 C chopped celery
- 2 cloves garlic, pressed
- 4 large tomatoes, chopped
- 8 oz tomato sauce
- 1/2 tsp pepper
- 2 tsp shredded fresh lemon peel
- 1/16 tsp cloves
- 1 bay leaf
- 1 tsp thyme
- 1 tsp honey
- 3 T parsley

In a large saucepan, sauté onion, green pepper, zucchini, and celery till tender in butter. Add garlic & tomatoes, bring to a boil. Reduce heat & add tomato sauce, pepper, lemon peel, cloves, bay, thyme, and honey. Simmer 15-20 minutes, stir frequently. Stir in shrimp & heat thoroughly. Serve over hot rice. Add hot pepper sauce if desired.

Shrimp and Grits/Classic Charleston Breakfast Shrimp

"This is what most Charlestonians think of as shrimp and grits. The secret to a nonpasty gravy is to cook the flour, which takes about 5 minutes. Even the largest shrimp need only cook for 3 minutes."

- 1 cup (1/2 pound) peeled shrimp
- 2 T (1/8 c) fresh lemon juice
- salt and cayenne pepper to taste
- 3 T bacon grease
- 1 small onion, finely chopped (about 1/4 c) about 1/4 c finely chopped green bell pepper 2 T (1/8 c) unbleached all-purpose flour
- 3/4 to 1 c hot water or stock (shrimp, chicken, or vegetable)
- Grits

In a bowl, sprinkle the shrimp with lemon juice, salt, and cayenne and set aside. Heat the bacon grease in a skillet and saute the onion and pepper over medium heat until the onion begins to become transparent, about 10 min. Sprinkle the flour over the vegetables and stir constantly for about 2 min, until the flour begins to brown.

Add the shrimp and about 3/4 c of water or stock, stirring constantly and turning the shrimp so that they cook evenly. Cook for another 2 to 3 minutes, until the shrimp are cooked through and the gravy is uniformly smooth, thinning with a little extra water or stock if necessary. Serve immediately over the grits.

Biscuit Topped Seafood Gumbo Pie

Gumbo:

- 3 tablespoons plus 1 teaspoon vegetable oil
- 3 tablespoons all-purpose flour
- 3 tablespoons butter
- 3/4 pound smoked sausage, sliced
- 3/4 pound cooked boneless ham steak, cut into 2 by 1/4 inch strips
- 1 large onion, chopped
- 2 garlic cloves, minced
- 1/2 green bell pepper, chopped
- 1/2 red bell pepper, chopped
- 1 small celery rib, minced
- 3 tablespoons rice
- 2 cups chicken stock
- 2 teaspoons fresh lemon juice
- 1/2 teaspoon cayenne pepper
- 3/4 pound shrimp, shelled
- 1/2 pound okra, sliced
- salt and freshly ground black pepper

Biscuit topping:

- 2 cups all-purpose flour
- 1 tablespoon baking powder
- 2 teaspoons sugar
- 1/2 teaspoon baking soda

- 1/2 teaspoon salt
- 6 1/2 tablespoons cold butter
- 3/4 cup buttermilk

Make the gumbo: In a heavy medium skillet, combine 3 tablespoons of the oil with the flour and cook over moderately low heat, stirring occasionally, until the roux is dark mahogany in color, about 1 hour. Do not let burn. Immediately remove from heat. In a medium flameproof casserole, melt 2 tablespoons of the butter with the Remaining 1 teaspoon oil. Add the sliced sausage and cook over moderate heat until well browned, about 5 minutes. Transfer to a plate with a slotted spoon. Add the ham strips to the casserole and cook until lightly browned, about 7 minutes; add to the plate with the sausage slices.

Add the remaining 1 tablespoon butter and the onion to the casserole. Cook over moderate heat, stirring constantly, until softened and translucent, about 2 minutes. Reduce the heat to moderately low and add the garlic

Creamy butter shrimp

- 1/2 oz. Parmigiano Reggiano) grated
- 2 tbsp. Almond Flour
- 1/2 tsp. Baking Powder
- 1/4 tsp. Curry Powder
- 1 tbsp. Water
- 1 large Egg
- 12 medium Shrimp
- 3 tbsp. Coconut Oil

Creamy Butter Sauce

- 2 tbsp. Unsalted Butter
- 1/2 small Onion, diced
- 1 clove Garlic, finely chopped
- 2 small Thai Chilies, sliced

Garnish

- 2 tbsp. Curry Leaves
- 1/2 cup Heavy Cream
- 1/3 oz. Mature Cheddar
- Salt and Pepper to Taste
- 1/8 tsp. Sesame Seeds

1. Remove the shells of the shrimps but leave the tail part if you'd like
2. Pat the cleaned shrimps dry with paper towels.

3. In a bowl, add 0.5 oz. grated Parmigiano Reggiano, 2 tbsp. almond flour, 1/2 tsp. baking powder and 1/4 tsp. curry powder (optional). Mix well. Gently cut the surface of the shrimps and devein. Clean well Into the mixture, add in 1 egg and 1 tbsp. water. Mix well until smooth.

4. Preheat a pan on medium heat. Add in 3 tsbp. coconut oil. Once the oil is hot, generously coat the shrimps with the batter and pan-fry the shrimps. Do these two to three at a time.

5. Wait until the shrimps turn golden brown and then remove them from the pan. Put on a cooling rock. Pan-fry extra batter if any left.

6. Preheat a pan to medium-low heat. Add in 2 tbsp. unsalted butter. Once the butter has melted, add in 1/2 chopped onion.

7. Wait until the onion turns translucent and then add in finely chopped garlic, sliced Thai chilies and 2 tbps. Curry leaves. Stir-fry everything until fragrant.

8. Add in the battered shrimp and coat well with the sauce.

9. Garnish with sesame seeds and serve! Goes well with cauliflower fried rice.

Prosciutto wrapped shrimp

- 10 oz. Pre-Cooked Shrimp
- 11 slices Prosciutto
- 1/3 cup Blackberries, Ground
- 1/3 cup Red Wine
- 2 tbsp. Olive Oil
- 1 tbsp. Mint Leaves, Chopped
- 1-2 tbsp. NOW Erythritol (to taste)

THE EXECUTION

1. Preheat your oven to 425F. Slice prosciutto in half or in thirds, depending on how many shrimp you have and their size. Wrap shrimp in prosciutto, starting from the tail and working your way up. Lay on a baking sheet, drizzle with 2 tbsp. olive oil, and cook for 15 minutes.

2. In a spice grinder, grind 1/3 cup Blackberries.

3. In a pan, add the blackberry puree and mint leaves. Add 1-2 tbsp. erythritol, to your tastes, then let cook for 2-3 minutes.

Add 1/3 cup red wine to the sauce and mix well. Then let reduce under simmer. Taste when reduced and add more sweetener if needed.

Serve with sauce on the side or drizzled over!

This will make about 4 single servings.
Each serving comes out to 247 Calories, 12.8g Fats,
1g Net Carbs, and 13.8g Protein

Thai peanut shrimp curry

- 2 tbsp. Green Curry Paste
- 1 cup Vegetable Stock
- 1 cup Coconut Milk
- 6 oz. Precooked Shrimp
- 5 oz. Broccoli Florets
- 3 tbsp. Cilantro, chopped
- 2 tbsp. Coconut Oil
- 1 tbsp. Peanut Butter
- 1 tbsp. Soy Sauce (or coconut Aminos)
- Juice of 1/2 Lime
- 1 medium Spring Onion, chopped
- 1 tsp. Crushed Roasted Garlic
- 1 tsp. Minced Ginger
- 1 tsp. Fish Sauce
- 1/2 tsp. Turmeric
- 1/4 tsp. Xanthan Gum
- 1/2 cup Sour Cream (for topping)

THE EXECUTION
1. Start by adding 2 tbsp. coconut oil in a pan over medium heat.
2. When the coconut oil is melted and the pan is hot, add the 1 tsp. Roasted garlic, 1 tsp. minced ginger, and 1 spring onion (chopped). Allow to cook for about a minute, then add 1 tbsp. green curry paste, and 1/2 tsp. turmeric.

3. Add 1 tbsp. soy sauce (or coconut Aminos), 1 tsp. fish sauce, and 1 tbsp. peanut butter to the pan and mix together well.

4. Add 1 cup of vegetable stock and 1 cup of coconut milk (from the carton). Stir well and then add another 1 tbsp. green curry paste.

5. Let simmer for a few minutes. In the meantime, measure out 6 oz. pre- cooked shrimp.

6. Add 1/4 tsp. xanthan gum to the curry and mix well.

7. Once your curry begins thickening up a little bit, add the broccoli florets and stir well.

8. Chop 3 tbsp. fresh cilantro and add to the pan.

9. Finally, once you are happy with the consistency of the curry, add the shrimp and lime juice from 1/2 lime, and mix everything together.

10. Let simmer for a few minutes. Taste and season with salt and pepper if needed.

11. Serve! You can stir in 1/4 cup of sour cream per serving.